ExcelTips

Excel 2003 Custom Formats

Compiled from the pages of ExcelTips, *your free weekly productivity newsletter*

tips.NET

Excel 2003 Custom Formats

Published by:

Sharon Parq Associates, Inc.
PO Box 794
Orem, UT 84059

Produced and published in the United States of America

Revision history:

4 Feb 2009: First published, e-book
2 Feb 2011: Excel 2003 version, e-book on CD (ISBN 978-1-61359-000-3)
2 Feb 2011: Excel 2003 version, e-book for download (ISBN 978-1-61359-001-0)
9 Feb 2011: Excel 2003 version, printed book (ISBN 978-1-61359-008-9)

Table of Contents

Introduction v

A Word about Versions vi

Need More Tips? vii

Custom Formatting Basics 1

Understanding Custom Formatting 1

Understanding Number Formatting Codes 3

Understanding Date and Time Formatting Codes 5

Understanding Color and Conditional Formatting Codes 6

Adding a Custom Format to those Offered by Excel 7

Saving Custom Formats 9

Creating Two-Line Custom Formats 10

Numeric Formatting 13

Displaying Negative Percentages in Red 13

Altering the Displayed Format of Numbers to the Nearest 100 16

Formatting Currency 17

Notation for Thousands and Millions 18

Entering Data as Thousands 19

Custom Formats for Scientific Notation 21

Incrementing Numeric Portions of Serial Numbers 22

Numbers in Base 12 23

Moving Custom Formats to Number Formatting Categories 24

Date and Time Formatting 25

Unique Date Displays 25
Entering Dates without Separators 27
Macro for Month Name 30
Entering Large Time Values 32
Displaying a Result as Minutes and Seconds 34
Formatting for Hundredths of Seconds 35
Dealing with Small Time Values 36
Using an Input Mask 37

Formatting Techniques and Ideas 41

Easy Value Hiding 41
Hiding Individual Cells 42
Using a Custom Format to Add Dashes 44
Partially Blocking Social Security Numbers 47
Superscripts in Custom Formats 48
Engineering Calculations 49
Inserting a Radical Symbol 53
Adjusting Cell Margins for More White Space 54
Labeling X-Y Scatter Plots 55

Introduction

One of the things that makes Excel so fun (and challenging) to work with is that you can do so much with it. In essence, Excel provides a wide range of individual building blocks that you can arrange in almost any way you desire to create your end result. There are literally hundreds of worksheet functions and scores of add-ins that can be combined in different ways to get just the results you want. Throw macros into the mix, and the sky is literally the limit when it comes to doing things with Excel.

One of the building blocks that is easy to overlook is custom formatting. This feature has been around since the earliest days of Excel, and it provides some amazing ways that you can affect the appearance of data in your worksheet. Custom formats are the basis for all the cell-level formatting that takes place in Excel; custom formats are combined in common ways and presented as the regular cell formats you know and use every day.

You can really extend your use of the program, however, if you take the time to understand how custom formats are implemented in Excel. Once you understand them, you are no longer limited to the common cell formats that you know and love. All of a sudden you've discovered a new set of building blocks that you can use to present your data in just the way you want.

The power of this elemental building block is the impetus behind *Excel 2003 Custom Formats*. In this e-book you'll discover a wide range of tips that can help you get a handle on how you can use custom formats in your workbooks. Brought to you by the publisher of *ExcelTips,* your free weekly productivity newsletter, this e-book zeroes in on what you need to know to understand and put custom formats to work right away.

The information presented in *Excel 2003 Custom Formats* is organized into a collection of bite-sized "tips" that have appeared in various issues of *ExcelTips*. In preparation for the publishing of this book the information in those tips have been carefully updated to reflect how to use best use custom formatting and to better convey what custom formats can do for you.

A Word about Versions

Many people are very contented using Excel 97, Excel 2000, Excel 2002, or Excel 2003, even though these are not the "latest and greatest" versions of the software. Given that the name of this e-book is *Excel 2003 Custom Formats,* you might be questioning if this e-book will work with the version of Excel you use.

In a word, it should. As far as Excel features go, the custom formatting features of the program have been quite stable over the versions listed at the beginning of this section. The instructions and screen shots used in this e-book were all created on an Excel 2003 system, but that shouldn't stop the information from being of use to you if you are using one of the other versions. As you compare what is on your screen with what you see in this e-book, don't be surprised if there are small, cosmetic differences. If you run across discrepancies of a more serious nature (I don't think you will), I'd love you to e-mail me with the details. Send your message to allen@sharonparq.com.

There is, however, one group of Excel users who will not find the information in this e-book that useful: those who use the very latest versions of Excel—2007 and 2010. The user interface in these versions is completely different than in earlier versions. If you are a user of Excel 2007 or Excel 2010, check at the Tips.Net store and you can find a version of this e-book that will work better for your purposes:

`http://store.tips.net/`

Need More Tips?

If you want to stay in top Excel form, consider subscribing to *ExcelTips*. Your subscription is free; all you need is an e-mail account and you can receive a weekly dose of tips related to Excel. To subscribe, just visit the *ExcelTips* Web site:

`http://excel.tips.net`

If you prefer to only consider tips that work with Excel 2007 or Excel 2010, then you'll want to visit our website that focuses on those versions:

`http://excelribbon.tips.net`

ExcelTips is part of the Tips.Net network, a collection of websites designed to bring you helpful tips, tricks, and ideas that can save you time, effort, and money. You can see the full breadth of the Tips.Net network by visiting our website:

`http://www.tips.net`

1

Custom Formatting Basics

Understanding Custom Formatting

Applies to Excel 97, 2000, 2002, and 2003

Excel allows you to format the information in your worksheet so that it appears just as you want it to appear. Most of the time, people use the formatting tools on Excel's toolbars and—in most cases—that type of formatting may be sufficient. However, Excel also allows you to create custom formats that provide you with even greater control over how your information is displayed.

Custom formatting is implemented by defining a pattern for how your data should appear. This pattern is entered in the Format Cells dialog box. Follow these steps:

1. Select the cell (or cells) that you want to format.
2. Choose Cells from the Format menu. Excel displays the Format Cells dialog box.
3. If the Number tab is not displayed, select it.
4. In the Category list, choose Custom. The dialog box changes so you can enter a custom format.

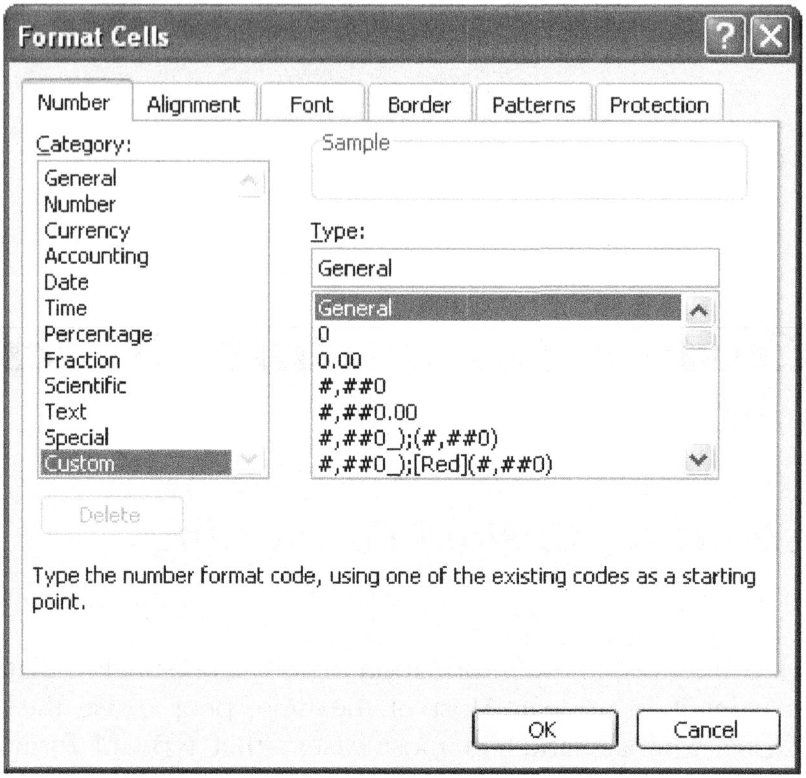

The Number tab of the Format Cells dialog box.

5. In the Type box, enter the pattern you want used for your custom format.
6. Click OK.

That's it; the pattern you specify in step 5 is used to display information in the cells selected in step 1.

Formatting patterns can look quite complex, especially to those who have not used them before. They aren't that hard, however, once you get the hang of them. There are four possible parts to a formatting pattern, each separated by a semicolon. The first part describes how a positive value should be displayed, the second a negative value, the third a zero value, and the fourth a text value. Only the first part of the formatting pattern is mandatory.

The following is an example of a pattern that shows numbers should be displayed with two decimal points and, if necessary, with a leading zero:

```
0.00
```

If you want to indicate that negative values should be shown in red, then you could use this format:

```
0.00;[Red]0.00
```

Note the use of the semicolon to separate the positive formatting and negative formatting patterns. When putting together the formatting pattern to be used by Excel, you should use the formatting codes described in later tips in this e-book.

Understanding Number Formatting Codes

Applies to Excel 97, 2000, 2002, and 2003

The most frequently used formatting codes are those that affect straight numbers. Excel provides many of them, as shown here:

Symbol	Meaning
General	Uses the general display format.
#	Indicates a single-digit position. The digit is only displayed if there is a digit in that position.
0	Indicates a single-digit position. If there is no digit in the position, a 0 is displayed.
?	Same as the 0 symbol, except results in a space being displayed for insignificant 0s on either side of the decimal point.
. (period)	The decimal point.
%	Percentage. The number is multiplied by 100 (for the display) and the % sign is added.
, (comma)	Thousands separator (if surrounded by digit place holders) or a thousands scalar (if the comma follows all the place holders).
E– E+ e– e+	Displays in scientific format.
$ – + / ( ) : space	Displays that character
\	Forces display of the following character
*	Repeats the next character to fill out the column width.

Symbol	Meaning
_ (underscore)	Leaves a space the width of the following character.
"text"	Displays the text within the quotes.
@	Text place holder.

To understand better what these codes do, take a look at the information in the following table, which shows several common formats and how they affect numbers.

Category	Format	Value	Displayed As
Number	#,##0.00	.01	0.01
		.1	0.10
		1234	1,234.00
		-5678	-5,678.00
Percentage	0.00%	.01	1.00%
		.1	10.00%
		1.234	123.40%
		-5.678	–567.80%
Scientific	0.00E+00	.01	1.00E-02
		.1	1.00E-01
		1234	1.23E+03
		-5678	–5.68E+03
Currency	$#,##0.00_);[Red]($#,##0.00)	.01	$0.01
		.1	$0.10
		1234	$1,234.00
		-5678	($5,678.00)

No matter which format is used to display numbers, the actual accuracy of the number is not affected. Thus, if a number is displayed using two decimal places, it is still maintained internally to 15 decimal places. All calculations are performed using the more accurate internal representation.

Understanding Date and Time Formatting Codes

Applies to Excel 97, 2000, 2002, and 2003

In Excel, dates and times are stored internally as numbers. These are only converted to legible dates and times when you format the cell using a date or time format. The following table lists the formatting codes that are specific to dates and times. You use these codes when you are creating a custom display format (Format | Cells | Number tab | Custom).

Symbol	Meaning
m	Displays the month or minutes as a number without a leading 0
mm	Displays the month or minutes as a number with a leading 0
mmm	Displays the month as abbreviated text (Jan, Feb, Mar, and so on)
mmmm	Displays the month as text (January, February, March, and so on)
d	Displays the day of the month as a number without a leading 0
dd	Displays the day of the month as a number with a leading 0
ddd	Displays the day of the week as abbreviated text (Sun, Mon, Tue, and so on)
dddd	Displays the day of the week as text (Sunday, Monday, Tuesday, and so on)
yy	Displays the year with two digits
yyyy	Displays the year with four digits
h	Displays the hour without a leading 0
hh	Displays the hour with a leading 0
s	Displays the seconds without a leading 0
ss	Displays the seconds with a leading 0
[ ]	When surrounding hours, minutes, or seconds place holders, displays hours greater than 24 or minutes and seconds greater than 60
AM am PM pm A a P p	Uses a 12-hour clock, displaying AM or PM as specified
\	Forces display of the following character
. (period)	The decimal point.
"text"	Displays the text within the quotes.

To understand better the effect of the date and time codes, take a look at the following information, which shows several common date and time formats and how they affect numbers.

Category	Format	Value	Displayed As
Date	m/d/yy	34369	2/4/94
	d-mmm-yy	34409	16-Mar-94
Time	h:mm AM/PM	0.654166667	3:42 PM
	[h]:mm:ss	2.592673611	62:13:27

Notice that the numbers shown in the value column of these examples are the internal values stored by Excel for dates and times.

Understanding Color and Conditional Formatting Codes

Applies to Excel 97, 2000, 2002, and 2003

In other issues of *ExcelTips* you learn how formatting codes are used to create custom formats used to display numbers, dates, and times. Excel also provides formatting codes to specify text display colors, as well as codes that indicate conditional formats. These formats only use a specific format when the value being displayed meets a certain criteria. To understand these codes a bit better, take a look at this format within the Currency category:

```
$#,##0.00_);[Red]($#,##0.00)
```

Notice there are two number formats divided by a semicolon. If there are two formats like this, Excel assumes that the one on the left is to be used if the number is 0 or above, and the one on the right is to be used if the number is less than 0. This example results in all numbers having a dollar sign, a comma being used as a thousands separator, amounts less than $1.00 having a leading 0, and negative values being shown in red with surrounding parentheses. The _) part of the left format is used so that positive and negative numbers align properly (positive numbers will leave a space the same width as a right parenthesis after the number).

You are not limited to only two formats. You can actually use four formats, each separated by a semicolon. The first is used if the value is above 0, the second is used if it is below 0, the third is used if it is equal to 0, and the fourth is used if the value being displayed is text.

The following table shows the color and conditional formatting codes. As you may have surmised, these codes are used with the formatting codes discussed in other issues of *ExcelTips*.

Symbol	Effect
[Black]	Black type.
[Blue]	Blue type.
[Cyan]	Cyan type.
[Green]	Green type.
[Magenta]	Magenta type.
[Red]	Red type.
[White]	White type.
[Yellow]	Yellow type.
[COLOR x]	Type in color code x, where x can be any value from 1 to 56.
[= value]	Use this format only if the number equals this value.
[< value]	Use this format only if the number is less than this value.
[<= value]	Use this format only if the number is less than or equals this value.
[> value]	Use this format only if the number is greater than this value.
[>= value]	Use this format only if the number is greater than or equals this value.
[<> value]	Use this format only if the number does not equal this value.

Adding a Custom Format to those Offered by Excel

Applies to Excel 97, 2000, 2002, and 2003

When you display the Format Cells dialog box (Format | Cells) and click Custom on the Number tab, Excel displays a list of custom formats. Some of these formats are provided by Excel by default, and others reflect custom formats used within the current workbook.

If you spend some time developing a custom format, it would be helpful to have that format always appear in the list of custom formats, regardless of which workbook you are using. Unfortunately, that is not in the cards for Excel; it lists only those custom formats unique to the current workbook.

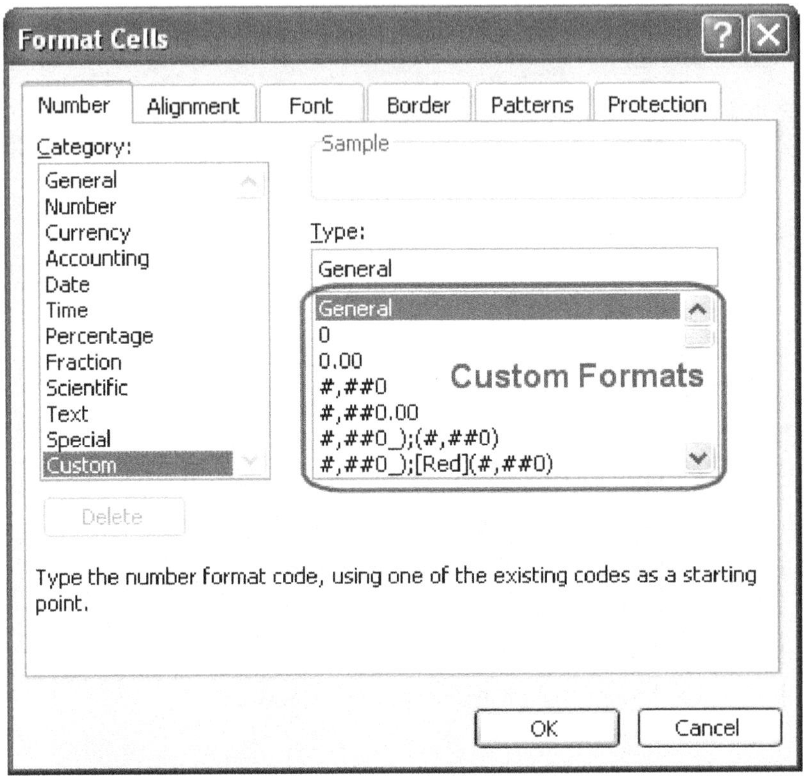

The Number tab of the Format Cells dialog box.

There are a couple of workarounds, however. The first is a natural extension to what is already mentioned in this tip—that the custom list includes any custom formats that have been defined in the current workbook. This means that you could replace Excel's default workbook with one of your own, and the custom format will be available in the list provided the format was defined in the workbook you saved as the default.

Sound confusing? It doesn't need to; all you need to do is start with a brand new workbook and define the custom format. Then, save the workbook as a template under the name Book.xlt, in the XLStart folder. (Just use Windows'

Search tool to look locate the XLStart folder.) This file (Book.xlt) then becomes the basis for all new workbooks, which means the custom format will be available in them. It will not affect any existing workbooks.

One problem with using the default-workbook approach is that the custom format, while included in the list, is at the bottom of the list. Unfortunately, there is no way to get your own preferred set of custom formats at the top of the list. There is a quick way to get exactly the custom formats you want, however—use macros.

Seriously, you can create a macro that applies a custom format of any desired type. The macro can be stored with individual workbooks or stored in the Personal.xls workbook so it is available to all workbooks on a system. You can use shortcut keys with the macro so that the format can be applied with a single keypress, or you can assign the macro to a toolbar button or custom menu so that it can be applied using the mouse.

Saving Custom Formats

Applies to Excel 97, 2000, 2002, and 2003

Excel provides quite a bit of flexibility in creating custom formats for cells in a workbook. In fact, depending on the needs of your data, you can spend quite a bit of time formatting cells so they look the way you want them to.

At some point you may get tired of doing the same formatting over and over again, and begin to wonder if there is a way to save your custom formats so you don't have to redefine them all the time. Unfortunately, there is not a full-featured way to save formats within Excel. You can get around this shortcoming quite easily, however. The trick is to define the cell formats as you want them, and then save the workbook as a template that you can later use as a basis for your future workbooks. All you need to do is use the Save As command and make sure the File Type drop-down list (at the bottom of the Save As dialog box) is set to Template.

As has been described in other issues of *ExcelTips,* you could replace your default workbook template with the new template you create, and then it becomes the basis for all new workbooks. All you need to do is give the template the name Book.xlt and save it in the XLStart folder. (The XLStart folder is in different places on different systems; use the searching capabilities of Windows to locate where it is on yours.)

Creating Two-Line Custom Formats

Applies to Excel 97, 2000, 2002, and 2003

Excel is quite flexible in how it allows you to set up custom formats for displaying all sorts of values. Most custom formats are straightforward and easy to figure out, once you understand how custom formats work.

What if you want to create a two-line custom format, however? For instance, you may want to format a date so that the abbreviated day of the week and day of the month is on the first line, followed by the unabbreviated name of the month on the second line. Using such a format, a date would appear in a single cell in this manner:

```
Sat 4
March
```

Most of this can be done by the custom format "ddd d mmmm", but you need to figure out a way to add a line break between the "d" and the "mmmm". Excel won't let you press **ALT+ENTER** between them, which is what you normally do to add a line break.

The solution is to use the numeric keypad to enter the desired line break in the format. Follow these steps to set it up:

1. Select the cells you want to format.
2. Choose Cells from the Format menu. Word displays the Format Cells dialog box.
3. Make sure the Number tab is selected.
4. In the Category list, choose Custom.

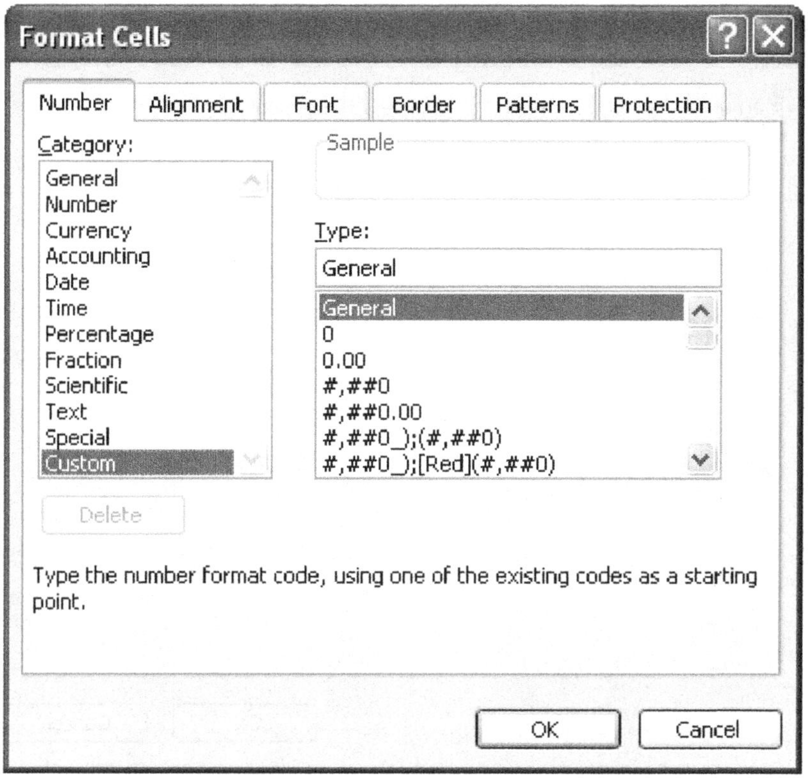

The Number tab of the Format Cells dialog box.

5. Delete whatever is in the Type box.
6. Type "ddd d" without the quote marks.
7. Hold down the **Alt** key while you press **0010** on the numeric keypad. This enters the line feed character, and it looks like the portion of the format you typed in step 6 disappears. It is not really gone; it has just moved up above what can be displayed in the Type box.
8. Type "mmmm" without the quote marks.
9. Click the Alignment tab.

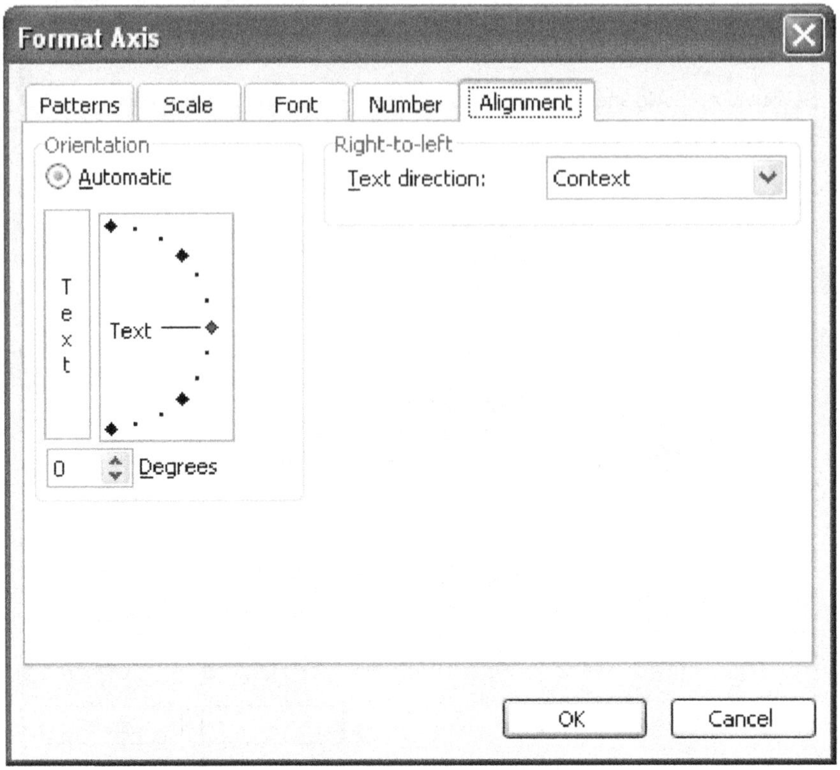

The Alignment tab of the Format Cells dialog box.

10. Make sure the Wrap Text check box is selected.
11. Click OK.

After setting up the format in this manner, you will need to adjust the row height of the formatted cells so that the entire two lines of the date will display.

2

Numeric Formatting

Displaying Negative Percentages in Red

Applies to Excel 97, 2000, 2002, and 2003

It's easy using Excel's built-in number formats to display negative values in red. What isn't so obvious is how to display negative percentages in red. This is because Excel doesn't provide a built-in format that addresses this situation.

There are two distinct ways you can display negative percentages in red. One way is to use a custom number format. Precise details on how you put together custom formats are covered elsewhere in this e-book, so here is the quick way you can get the desired results:

1. Select the cell (or cells) that may contain negative percentages.
2. Choose Cells from the Format menu. Excel displays the Format Cells dialog box.
3. If the Number tab is not displayed, select it.
4. In the Category list, choose Custom. The dialog box changes so you can enter a custom format.

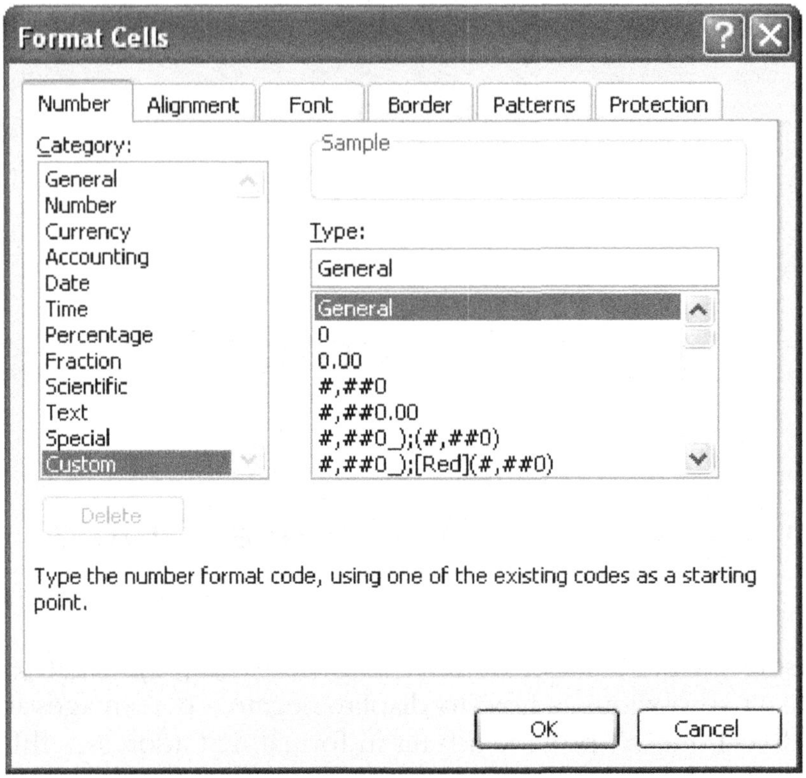

The Number tab of the Format Cells dialog box.

5. In the Type box, enter the following: **0.00%;[Red]-0.00%**
6. Click OK.

The format you specify in step 5 displays positive percentages with two decimal places and displays negative percentages in red with two decimal places. (You can modify the number of decimal places in the format, if necessary.)

The other way that you can display negative percentages in red is to use conditional formatting. Follow these steps:

1. Select the cell (or cells) that may contain negative percentages.
2. Choose Conditional Formatting from the Format menu. Excel displays the Conditional Formatting dialog box.

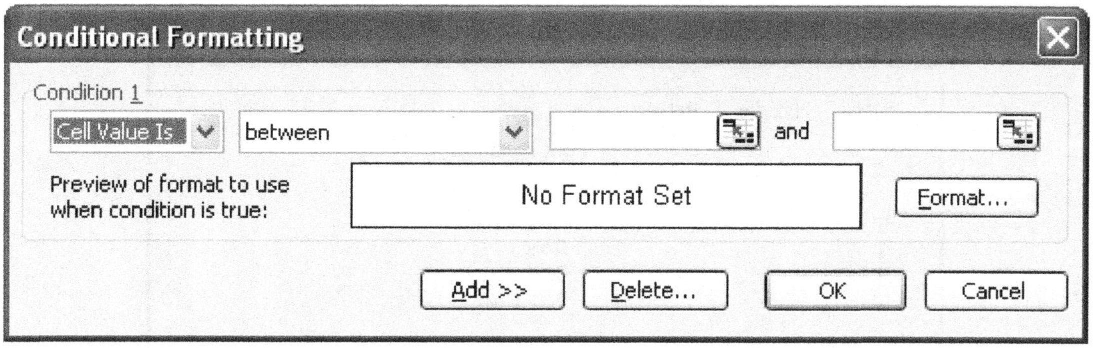

The Conditional Formatting dialog box.

3. Leave the first drop-down list set to Cell Value Is.
4. Change the second drop-down list to Less Than.
5. In the box to the right of the second drop-down list, enter the numeral 0.
6. Click Format. Excel displays the Format Cells dialog box with the Font tab selected.

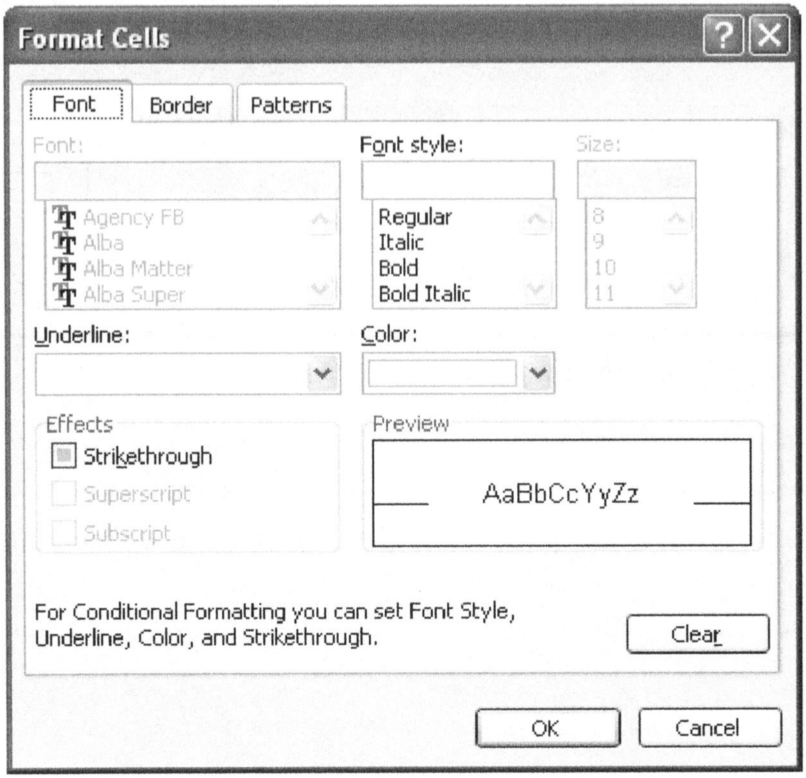

The Font tab of the Format Cells dialog box.

7. Use the Color drop-down list to choose the shade of red you want used for the negative percentages.
8. Click OK to close the Format Cells dialog.
9. Click OK to close the Conditional Formatting dialog.

Altering the Displayed Format of Numbers to the Nearest 100

Applies to Excel 97, 2000, 2002, and 2003

Frank asked if there is a way, using a custom number format, to round the display of numbers to the nearest 10, 100, etc., without affecting the original numbers.

The answer is that there is a way and there isn't a way. (Don't you love those answers?) There are custom number formats that allow you to round the display to the nearest thousand or the nearest million, as follows:

```
[<=500] "0";#,"000"
[<=500000] "0";#,,"000000"
```

The first format will round to the nearest thousand, and the second will round to the nearest million. If you are looking for a custom format that will round to some other power of 10, you are out of luck, however. In those instances, the best solution may be to simply create another worksheet that uses formulas for rounding and uses the contents of the original worksheet as the source.

Formatting Currency

Applies to Excel 97, 2000, 2002, and 2003

Eric asked if there was a way to easily format cells so what would normally appear as $10,000.00 would appear as $10.000,00. This format being described is the difference between the US method of displaying figures (using commas as thousand separators and a period as a decimal sign) and the European method of displaying figures (using periods as thousand separators and a comma as a decimal sign).

There are three ways you can accomplish a switch. The easiest method is to simply change the Regional Settings in Windows. The exact way you do this depends on the version of Windows you are using, but in general there is a choice in the Windows Control Panel that allows you to specify regional settings. All you need to do is modify those settings to match the numeric display format desired. The change will affect not only the display of numbers in Excel, but in other Windows-compliant programs, as well.

The second method is to use a formula to handle the numeric display. This has the drawback of converting the numeric value to text, but it could be easily done. For instance, let's assume that you have the formatted numeric value $10,000.00 in cell A1. The following formula, in a different cell, would display the text $10.000,00:

```
=SUBSTITUTE(SUBSTITUTE(SUBSTITUTE(TEXT(A1,
"$#,##0.00"),".","^"),",","."),"^",",")
```

This formula first converts the number to an initial currency format in text. Then the SUBSTITUTE function is used to first change "." to "^" ("^" is used as a temporary placeholder), and then change "," to ".", and finally "^" to ",".

The final method has the advantage of leaving your numbers as numbers, instead relying on a custom format. All you need to do is to multiply your values by 100 and then use the following custom format:

```
#"."###"."###","##
```

The format allows any number up to 9.999.999,00 to be used. If you deal with numbers that have more than two decimal places, you will need to adjust your custom format accordingly, or adjust the value being displayed so that it has nothing to the right of the decimal point after it is multiplied by 100.

Notation for Thousands and Millions

Applies to Excel 97, 2000, 2002, and 2003

Jim wonders how he can get Excel to automatically display numbers using "k" for thousands and "m" for millions. As an example, if a cell contains the value $470,000 he would like it displayed as $470k; if it contains the value $1,107,432 he would like it displayed as $1.1m.

One obvious method is to create a formula that will display the information as desired. The following formula will take into account the magnitude of the number in cell B2 and then provide a formatted text string appropriate to that magnitude:

```
=IF(B2 < 1000,B2,IF(B2 < 1000000,
"$" & ROUND(B2/1000,1) & "k",
"$" & ROUND(B2/1000000,1) & "m"))
```

Remember that this is a single formula and should be entered entirely on one line. The drawback with such an approach, of course, is that the formula takes up space within your worksheet. To get around this you could, instead, create a custom format that will simply affect the display of the number in the cell.

To create a custom format, choose Cells from the Format menu, display the Number tab, and click Custom at the left side of the dialog box. Here's the custom format you should actually use:

```
[>1000000]$#.0,,"m";[>1000]$#,"k";$#,##0
```

This format will display both millions and thousands using the desired notation. If the number is below a thousand then it will be displayed without any special notation. As appropriate, values are rounded to one decimal place.

Entering Data as Thousands

Applies to Excel 97, 2000, 2002, and 2003

Richard would like to type a value into a cell and have Excel assume that the value is thousands. For instance, he would like to enter "3" into a cell and have Excel treat the value as 3,000; if he enters "14" into the cell, then Excel should treat it as 14,000.

There are several different ways that this can be handled, depending on how you want the data treated once it is entered. One approach is to change the formatting of the cell into which the values are being entered. You could, for instance, use the following custom format for the cell:

```
#,##0",000"
```

Whenever you enter a value in the cell, Excel follows the value with ",000". Thus, enter 27 in the cell and Excel displays 27,000.

The drawback to this approach is that the underlying number is still considered the smaller value. If you later try to add 1 to the cell contents, you don't get 27,001, you get 28,000. You also won't be able to enter decimal values. This means that if you enter 1.23, you don't get 1,230; you instead get 1,000 because the value is treated as an integer before displaying.

A better approach is, perhaps, to change a configuration setting in Excel itself. Follow these steps:

1. Choose Options from the Tools menu. Excel displays the Options dialog box.
2. Make sure the Edit tab is displayed.

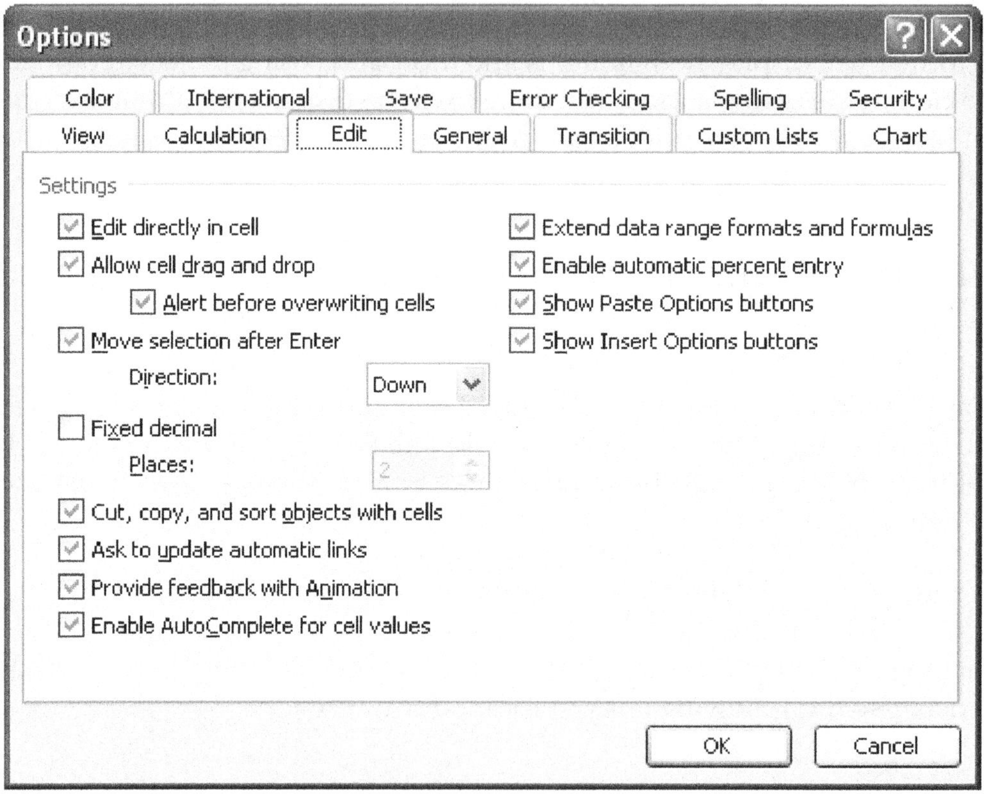

The Edit tab of the Options dialog box.

3. Check the Fixed Decimal Places check box and change the value at the right of the option to -3.
4. Click OK.

Now, whenever you enter any information into a cell, Excel automatically multiplies the value by 1,000, provided you don't include a decimal point in what you are entering. This means that if you enter the value 3, Excel actually enters 3,000 into the cell. If you instead enter 1.23, then Excel enters 1.23; it doesn't multiply by 1,000.

If you choose this approach, remember that it is not only data entry on the current worksheet that is affected. This setting affects all data entry on all worksheets from this time forward. If this is not what you want, then you'll need to remember to turn off the setting (clear the check box) when you want to return to normal data entry.

You could, as well, use a macro approach to the problem. For instance, if you are entering only numeric data into the worksheet, you could create a macro that will multiply the contents of a cell by 1,000 every time the cell changes. Right-click the worksheet tab and choose View Code from the resulting Context menu. Then enter the following macro into the code window:

```
Private Sub Worksheet_Change(ByVal Target As Range)
    Application.EnableEvents = False
    Target = Target * 1000
    Application.EnableEvents = True
End Sub
```

Perhaps the best solution, though, is to keep things simple. Have a column where you input your values as you want. Then, in another column, use a formula to modify whatever values you entered. For example, you could enter 1.23 into cell A1. In cell B1, then, you could multiply this value by 1,000. The value in cell B1 could then be used within other formulas, elsewhere in your workbook.

Custom Formats for Scientific Notation

Applies to Excel 97, 2000, 2002, and 2003

Reid notes that he can display numbers using scientific notation and they appear in Excel in the format 1.23E+03 or 1.23E-03. He would like the scientific notation to be shown differently, such as 1.23x10^3 or 1.23x10^-3.

There is no way in Excel to change the way in which scientific notation is displayed. The only workaround is to use a formula to put together a text representation of what you want. For instance, if a value that uses Excel's scientific notation is stored in cell C7, you could use the following formula:

```
=LEFT(TEXT(D7,"0.00E+0"),3) & "x10^" & RIGHT(TEXT(D7,"0.00E+0"),3)
```

This formula essentially pulls the left portion of the number (the part before the E) and combines it with the right part of the number (the part after the E) together with the "x10^" notation. The result is considered a text string by Excel; it cannot be used in subsequent calculations.

If you needed to do quite a bit of formatting in this manner, it would be a relatively trivial matter to create a macro that returned the formatted text string based on the number. Create it as a user-defined function and you could then use it in your formulas.

Incrementing Numeric Portions of Serial Numbers

Applies to Excel 97, 2000, 2002, and 2003

Ted has a range of serial numbers in the format A12345678B. He would like to find a formula that will increment the numeric portion of the serial numbers by 1. Thus, the next number in sequence would be A12345679B, then A12345680B.

There are actually a couple of ways you can go about this, and the first doesn't really involve a formula at all. Instead you can create a custom format that displays your serial number. How you go about creating custom formats is described elsewhere in this e-book; the format should look like this:

```
"A"#"B"
```

Then, in a cell that has this format applied, you only need to include the numeric portion of the serial number (12345678). You can then use regular AutoFill techniques to fill out as many cells as necessary with the serial number.

If you have your heart set on using a formula, then the following should work just fine as long as the pattern for the serial number is a single letter, eight numeric digits, and a single terminating letter:

```
=LEFT(A1,1) & MID(A1,2,8)+1 & RIGHT(A1,1)
```

This assumes that cell A1 contains the beginning serial number. If you put the formula in cell A2, it could be copied down as many times as necessary for the desired number of serial numbers.

If the numeric portion of the serial number could start with leading zeroes, then you need to use a different formula to provide the proper zero padding:

```
=LEFT(A1,1) & TEXT(VALUE(MID(A1,2,8))+1,"00000000") & RIGHT(A1,1)
```

Numbers in Base 12

Applies to Excel 97, 2000, 2002, and 2003

For some professions or hobbies, it may be required to display information in "base 12." For instance, you may need to display the number of dozens of an item, followed by the number of singles of an item. If you had 15 items, for instance, you may want your display to be 1:03.

There are a couple of different ways to approach this problem. The first is to do the math and put together a string that represents the finished numbers. For instance, suppose the original number is in cell B7. In cell C9 you could place the following:

```
=INT(B7/12) & ":" & RIGHT("00" & MOD(B7,12),2)
```

In this instance, if B7 contained the number 345, C9 would contain the string 28:09. If you would rather work with straight numbers, you can use the following formula in cell C9:

```
=INT(B7/12)*100+MOD(B7,12)
```

In this case, cell C9 would contain 2809, which could be easily displayed in the final format by setting the custom number format for the cell as 0":"00.

Regardless of which approach you choose, you should know that you won't be able to use the results in any mathematical functions. The information displayed is done so solely for that purpose—display.

Moving Custom Formats to Number Formatting Categories

Applies to Excel 97, 2000, 2002, and 2003

Neil knows how to create custom formats in Excel. He has created a custom format that displays dates exactly as he wants them displayed and he would like this custom format to show up in the Date category (Number tab of the Format Cells dialog) rather than being left in the Custom category. Neil wonders if there is a way to do this.

The short answer is that no, there is no way to do this. The formats that appear in the non-custom categories are hard-coded by Excel. The only thing you could do to make the application of the custom formats faster (if that is your goal) is to use a macro that applies the format. The following is an example of a macro that applies a custom format to whatever cells are selected:

```
Sub MyNumberFormat()
    Selection.NumberFormat = "_(* #,##0_);_(* (#,##0);_(* ""-""??_);_(@_)"
End Sub
```

You can assign the macro to a shortcut key or to a button on a toolbar, thereby making it very easy to apply.

3

Date and Time Formatting

Unique Date Displays

Applies to Excel 97, 2000, 2002, and 2003

Jon requested help on how to subtract two dates and display the result such that the years were on the left of the decimal and the months on the right. Thus, if you subtracted January 7, 1985 from August 12, 2009, the result would be 24.7.

The easiest way to do this is to simply do your date subtractions as regular, and then use a custom format to display the result. For instance, if the lower date were in cell A2 and the higher date in B2, you could use the following formula in C2:

```
=B2-A2
```

You would then follow these steps to format the display of the result in cell C2:

1. Select the cell. (In this case, cell C2.)
2. Choose Cells from the Format menu. Excel displays the Format Cells dialog box.
3. Make sure the Number tab is selected.
4. In the Category list, at the left side of the dialog box, choose Custom.

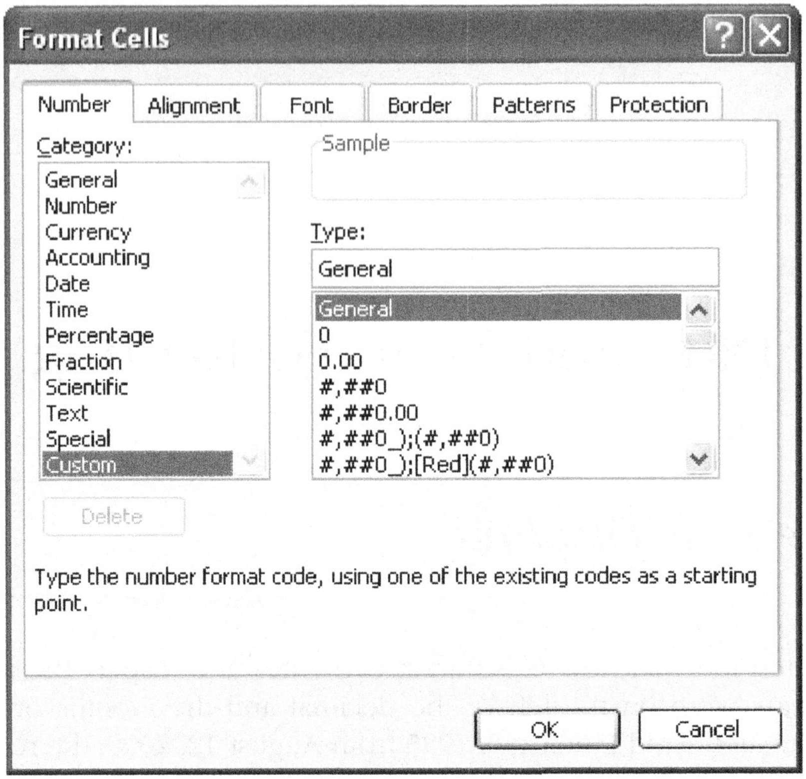

The Number tab of the Format Cells dialog box.

5. In the Type box, at the left of the dialog box, enter the following format: **yy.m**
6. Click on OK.

The result is that C2 shows the number of years to the left of the decimal and the number of months to the right. The problem with this is that it will always vary the number of months from 1 to 12, rather than 0 to 11, as one would expect if you were looking for elapsed months.

To overcome this, you could enter the following formula in cell C2:

```
=(YEAR(B2)-YEAR(A2))+(MONTH(B2)-MONTH(A2))/100
```

This formula returns the number of years on the left of the decimal and the number of months on the right. The months are always expressed using two decimal places, however. If you wanted to make sure that the months were expressed with no leading zeros, then you would use this formula variation:

```
=VALUE(ABS(YEAR(B2)-YEAR(A2)) & "." & ABS(MONTH(B2)-MONTH(A2)))
```

Entering Dates without Separators

Applies to Excel 97, 2000, 2002, and 2003

Different people enter data in different ways. When you enter information into a cell, Excel tries to figure out what type of information you are entering. If you enter a number such as 08242010, Excel assumes you are entering a numeric value, and treats it accordingly. What if the number you enter actually is a date, without any separators? Can Excel understand what you are entering?

Unfortunately Excel cannot. Why? Because you have given it no indication that this should be a date. (Excel keys on separators, not on numeric values.) If you or your data entry people cannot change their input habits so that separators are also entered, then you will need some sort of a workaround to convert the entered information to an actual date value.

Your first thought might be that you could use a custom format to display the information. Consider the following custom format:

```
##"/"##"/"####
```

This format would display the number 08152010 as 8/15/2010. The only problem is that it only changes the display of the number—if you want to use the date as a real Excel date, you cannot do so because you haven't converted the value into something that Excel recognizes as a date.

If the values input were very consistent in their format, and if they were input as text instead of as numeric values, then there is an easy way you can convert them to dates. By very consistent, I mean that the input always used two digits for the month, two for the day, and four for the year. In addition, the cells containing the values must be formatted as text. In this instance, you can follow these steps:

1. Select the column of dates.
2. Make sure there is nothing in the column just to the right of the dates.
3. Choose Text to Columns from the Data menu. Excel displays the Convert Text to Columns Wizard.

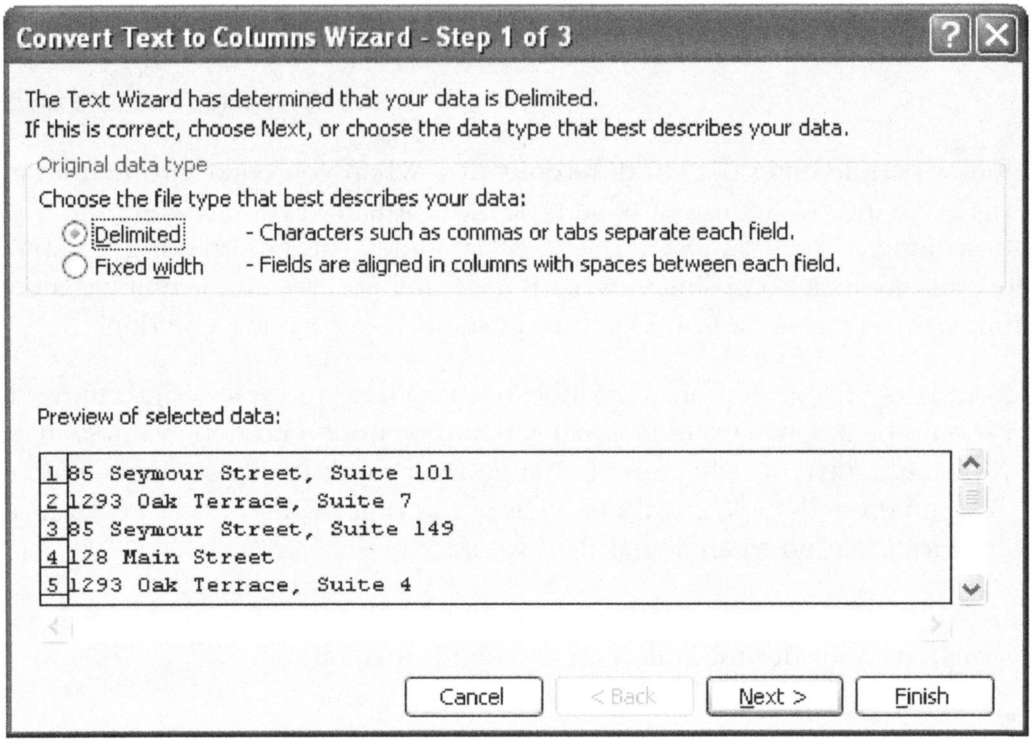

The Convert Text to Columns Wizard.

4. Select the Fixed Width option, then click on Next.
5. Click on Next again.
6. In the Column Data Format area, choose Date.
7. Select the range in the Destination box, then in the worksheet click the cell just to the right of the first value you selected in step 1.
8. Click on Finish.

If all went well, Excel should have parsed the text values as dates, and you can delete the original column. If this did not work, then it means that either the original values were not formatted as text, or eight digits were not used to enter all the dates.

Another possible solution is to use a formula to convert the entered values into actual dates. The following is one such formula:

```
=DATE(RIGHT(A1,4),LEFT(A1,IF(LEN(A1) = 8,2,1)),LEFT(RIGHT(A1,6),2))
```

This formula assumes that the entered date (the one without separators) is in cell A1. The formula will work with either seven- or eight-digit dates.

If you prefer custom functions, you can create one in VBA that examines the data being passed, converts it to a date/time format, and then returns the result. The following function is very versatile in this regard; it will work with both American and European date formats:

```
Function DateTime(dblDateTime As Double, _
  Optional bAmerican As Boolean = True)
'Converts Date and time "number" without
'delimiters into an excel serialdate (which
'can then be formatted with the Excel
'date/time formats)

'If optional argument is TRUE (or missing),
'function assumes value is of form:
'    [m]mddyyyy.hhmm  (leading "0" not required)

'If optional argument is FALSE, function
'assumes value is of form:
'    [d]dmmyyyy.hhmm  (leading "0" not required)

    Dim iYear As Integer
    Dim iMonth As Integer
    Dim iDay As Integer
    Dim iHour As Integer
    Dim iMin As Integer

    iYear = Int((dblDateTime / 10000 - _
      Int(dblDateTime / 10000)) * 10000)
    iDay = Int((dblDateTime / 1000000 - _
      Int(dblDateTime / 1000000)) * 100)
    iMonth = Int((dblDateTime / 1000000))
    iHour = Int((dblDateTime - Int(dblDateTime)) * 100)
    iMin = Int((dblDateTime * 100 - _
      Int(dblDateTime * 100)) * 100 + 0.5)

    If bAmerican Then
        DateTime = DateSerial(iYear, iMonth, iDay)
```

```
    Else
        DateTime = DateSerial(iYear, iDay, iMonth)
    End If

    DateTime = DateTime + (iHour + iMin / 60) / 24
End Function
```

This macro function assumes that the data being passed to it is a numeric value, as would normally happen when inputting dates without separators. (Refer back to the logic on this at the beginning of the tip.)

As you can tell, there are a number of workarounds, but none of them is as simple as just entering separators when entering the dates. If training yourself or your data input people to do this is difficult, you might consider setting up some data validation rules for the input cells. These rules can check to make sure that you are entering information using a specific format (such as a date with separators), and stop you if you are not. (How you create data validation rules has been covered in other issues of *ExcelTips*.)

Macro for Month Name

Applies to Excel 97, 2000, 2002, and 2003

Brian is looking for a macro that returns the full name of the current month, such as July, August, etc. Before getting to the macros, it should be mentioned that depending on your needs, you could get the desired information with one of several formulas. Perhaps the easiest formula is the following:

```
=Today()
```

Place the formula into a cell, and you end up with today's date. Format the cell using a custom format, and you end up with the full month name. The custom format is applied by using these steps:

1. Select the cell containing the formula.
2. Choose Cells from the Format menu. Excel displays the Format Cells dialog box.
3. Make sure the Number tab is displayed.

4. In the list of format categories, select Custom.

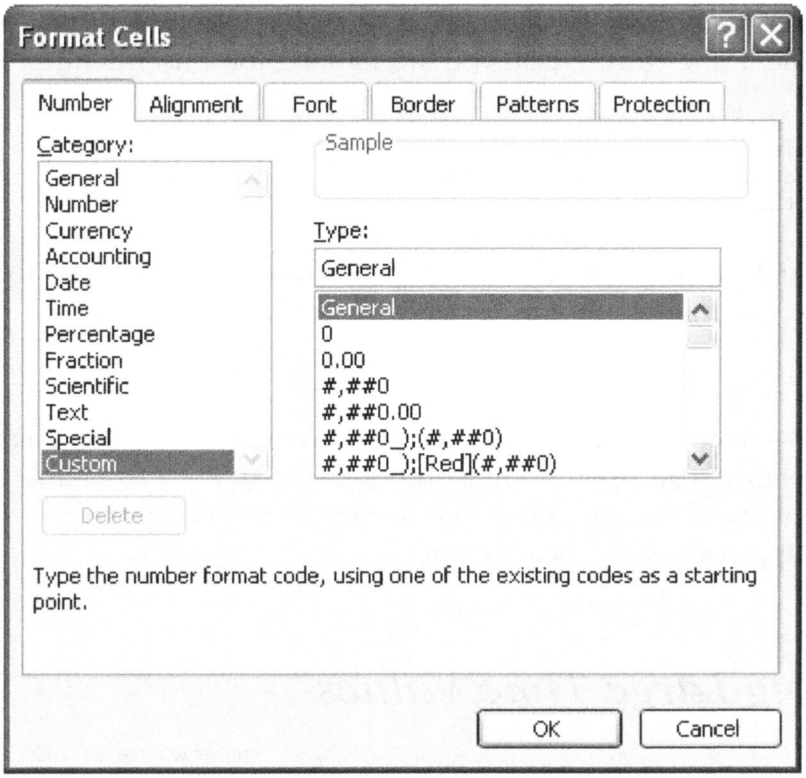

The Number tab of the Format Cells dialog box.

5. In the Type box, enter **mmmm**.
6. Click OK.

Another formulaic approach is to use the following in a cell:

```
=Text(Today(),"mmmm")
```

No special formatting is required; the formula returns the text of the full month name for whatever today is. Finally, you could use an even longer formula that simply picks the month name from a list of months:

```
=CHOOSE(MONTH(NOW()),"January","February",
"March","April","May","June","July",
"August","September","October","November",
"December")
```

Remember that this is a single formula; it goes all in one cell.

Which brings us, finally, to the macros. If you want a macro that returns the month name in the current cell, you are looking for a user-defined function:

```
Function MonthName()
    Application.Volatile
    MonthName = Format(Date, "mmmm")
End Function
```

This simple two-line macro dynamically returns the month name for whatever the current date is. Just put this formula in a cell:

```
=MonthName()
```

Remember—since you've just added a macro to your workbook, you'll be asked whenever you open your workbook if you want to enable macros. If you don't want to see this question all the time, you should use one of the formulaic approaches presented earlier.

Entering Large Time Values

Applies to Excel 97, 2000, 2002, and 2003

If you format a cell for elapsed time (using a custom display format of [h]:mm:ss), then Excel allows you to enter hours, minutes and seconds into that cell. For instance, you could simply enter 129:14:30 to signify 129 hours, 14 minutes, and 30 seconds. You run into a problem, however, if you try to enter very large time values into the cell. When you try to enter time values in excess of 10000 hours, as in 12721:52:45, then Excel won't parse the entry as a time, but treats it as text.

The interesting thing is that when a cell is formatted for elapsed time using [h]:mm:ss, the cell can easily display elapsed times that have more than 10000 hours. Thus, you can sum a range of cells to result in a value more than 10000 hours, but you cannot enter a larger value.

Unfortunately, there seems to be no way around this in Excel. The best solution, however, might be to rethink how the data is entered. After all, 10000 hours is equal to 416 days and 16 hours—well over a year. You could easily create a column for entering days, and use another for partial days. A third column could then use a formula to return the elapsed hours based on the other two columns.

Another solution is to simply not rely on Excel to do the parsing of your input. If you have a huge number of hours to enter (such as 32315), then you could enter the following in the cell:

```
=32315/24
```

Excel maintains what you enter as a formula, but displays the proper number of hours, minutes, and seconds. If you want to get more precise, you can enter a fractional amount that represents the portion of an hour represented by your time. For instance, 37 minutes and 15 seconds is 0.620833 of an hour. Thus, you could enter the hours as follows:

```
=32315.620833/24
```

Of course, entering times in this manner can get tedious, particularly when you have calculate the fractional portion of an hour represented by minutes and seconds. To overcome this, you could create a custom function that allows you to enter hours, minutes, and seconds, and returns a value that is easily formatted using the elapsed time format. The following function will do the trick:

```
Public Function RealBigTime(hr As Double, _
  min As Double, sec As Double) As Double
    Dim hr1 As Double
    Dim min1 As Double
    Dim sec1 As Double

    Application.Volatile
    hr1 = hr / 24
    min1 = min / 24 / 60
    sec1 = sec / 24 / 60 / 60
    RealBigTime = hr1 + min1 + sec1
End Function
```

After creating the function, enter something like =RealBigTime(32341,30,45) in a cell. The result is a value that can be formatted with the elapsed time format to 32341:30:45.

Displaying a Result as Minutes and Seconds

Applies to Excel 97, 2000, 2002, and 2003

When Deepak divides two numbers, he would like the result shown in minutes and seconds instead of a decimal value. For example, the result of the division 315/130 is 2.42 minutes, but he would like it displayed as 2:25 (2 minutes, 25 seconds).

Welcome to the wonder world of working with time values in Excel. You need to understand that Excel, intrinsically, works with decimal values—such as 2.42. (Actually dividing 315 by 130 results in an answer of 2.42307692.) There are several ways that you can display this as a non-decimal value, such as 2:25. One way is to use a formula such as the following, which returns a text value:

```
=TEXT(INT(315/130),"0") & ":" & TEXT((315/130-INT(315/130))*60,"0")
```

The problem with using such a formula, however, is that the resulting text value cannot be used in further calculations. (Well, not without jumping through bothersome and unnecessary hoops.) A better solution is to follow these general steps:

1. Divide the result (2.42307692) by 1440.
2. Select the cell with this result and format it to use the custom format **mm:ss**.

That's it. Your cell now shows 2:25, just as desired. Why does this work? It has to do with how Excel stores dates and times internally. Understand that, in Excel's world, anything to the left of the decimal point (2) is a number of days. Anything to the right of the decimal point (.42307692) is a portion of a full day. Thus, to get value 2.42307692 to something that Excel can understand as a number of minutes and seconds, you need to divide it by the number of minutes in a day (24 * 60, or 1440).

With the value "normalized" to what Excel expects for dates and times, you can then apply formatting to the cell and Excel displays it as you expect.

Formatting for Hundredths of Seconds

Applies to Excel 97, 2000, 2002, and 2003

Paolo wants to record times in an Excel workbook, but he needs the times to be precise, including hundredths of a second. What he would like is a format such as 1.41.73, meaning 1 minute, 41 seconds, and 73 hundredths.

This type of formatting can be easily applied to a cell in the following manner:

1. Select the cell or cells you want to format.
2. Choose Cells from the Format menu. Excel displays the Format Cells dialog box.
3. Make sure the Number tab is selected.
4. In the Category list, choose Custom.

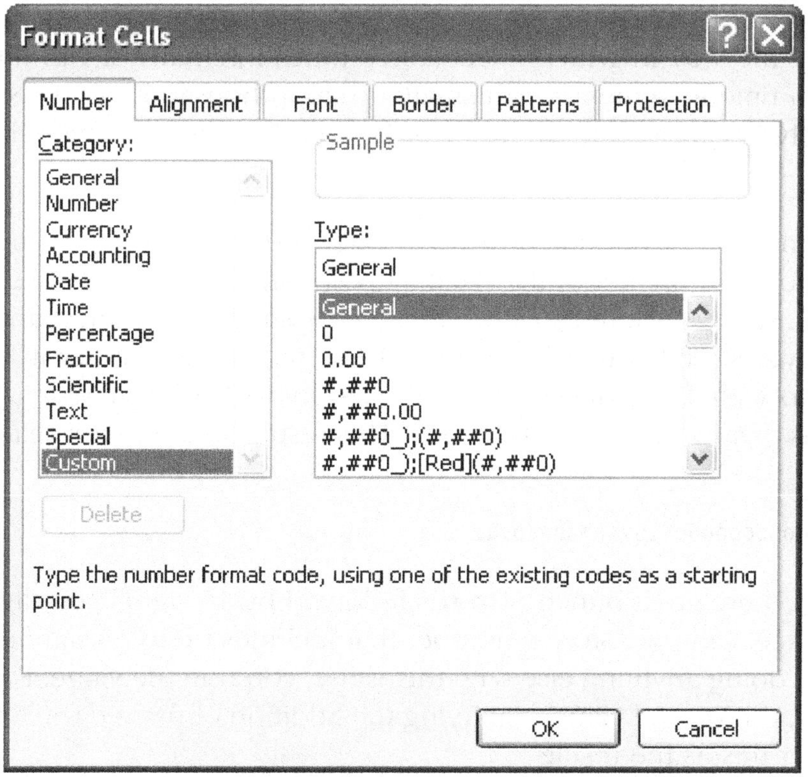

The Number tab of the Format Cells dialog box.

5. In the Type box, enter the following: **[h]:mm:ss.00**
6. Click OK.

The format shows elapsed time, with hours, minutes, seconds, and hundredths of seconds. If you prefer, you can change what delimiters are used between each element of the time. For instance, if you want to use decimal points and drop off the hours, you can use the following format in step 5: **mm.ss.00**.

Dealing with Small Time Values

Applies to Excel 97, 2000, 2002, and 2003

Zuzana has a need to perform calculations with very small time increments, such as thousandths of a second. She wonders how small of times Excel can deal with and how she can format for the display of the small increments.

Because of the way in which Excel stores times internally, it can theoretically deal with a time increment much smaller than a thousandth of a second. I say theoretically because there are a lot of factors that can negatively impact that precision.

As an example, consider that times and dates are stored in Excel such that full days are stored to the left of the decimal point and fractions of days are stored to the right. If you wanted to store a value as small as a hundred billionth of a second, you could conceivably do it. To store such a number in this format you end up with 1 day divided by 24 hours divided by 60 minutes divided by 60 seconds divided by 100,000,000,000. This results in a number that looks like this:

```
0.000000000000000115740740740741
```

Notice that there are a bunch of zeros followed by 15 significant digits. This is because Excel can only store a number that includes up to 15 significant digits. If you start doing anything else with this value, you ruin the value. For instance, you could add 3 to the value, signifying the addition of three days. Excel would then render this as the result:

```
3.000000000000000000000000000000
```

Notice that the small time increment disappeared. This happened because in the result of the addition, everything after the 3 became "significant," and Excel can only keep track of up to 15 significant digits, which was all zeros in the original number.

A thousandth of a second is a much longer duration than a hundred billionth of a second; it is represented in Excel's internal formatting as this:

```
0.0000000115740740740741
```

If you add three days to this value, you end up with this:

```
3.00000001157407
```

This is still accurate enough to render thousandths of a second just fine.

Of course, it doesn't do much good to store thousandths of a second internally if you can't display them in Excel. This is where custom formatting comes into play. You can create a custom format (as described in other issues of *ExcelTips*) that will display thousandths of a second just fine. Here's the format to use:

```
h:mm:s.000
```

If you try to use more zeros in the format (to display smaller increments of time), Excel will balk. The smallest increment you can display using custom formats is a thousandth of a second.

Using an Input Mask

Applies to Excel 97, 2000, 2002, and 2003

When inputting time into a cell, it is easy to enter digits—that's what the numeric keypad is for, after all. What can really slow you down is the necessity to enter other characters, particularly ones that require the use of the **Shift** key. For instance, if you are entering times, it is easy to enter 230 for 2:30, but it is a pain to slow down by entering the colon.

Thus, you may wonder if there is a way to set up an input mask that will add the colon automatically. The good news is yes, there is. The bad news is no, there isn't. Sound confusing? Let me explain...

You can set up a custom format that will display your time in any format you want. For instance, you could use the following steps:

1. Select the cells you want to use for time input.
2. Choose Cells from the Format tab. Excel display the Format Cells dialog box.
3. Make sure the Number tab is selected.
4. In the Category list, choose Custom.

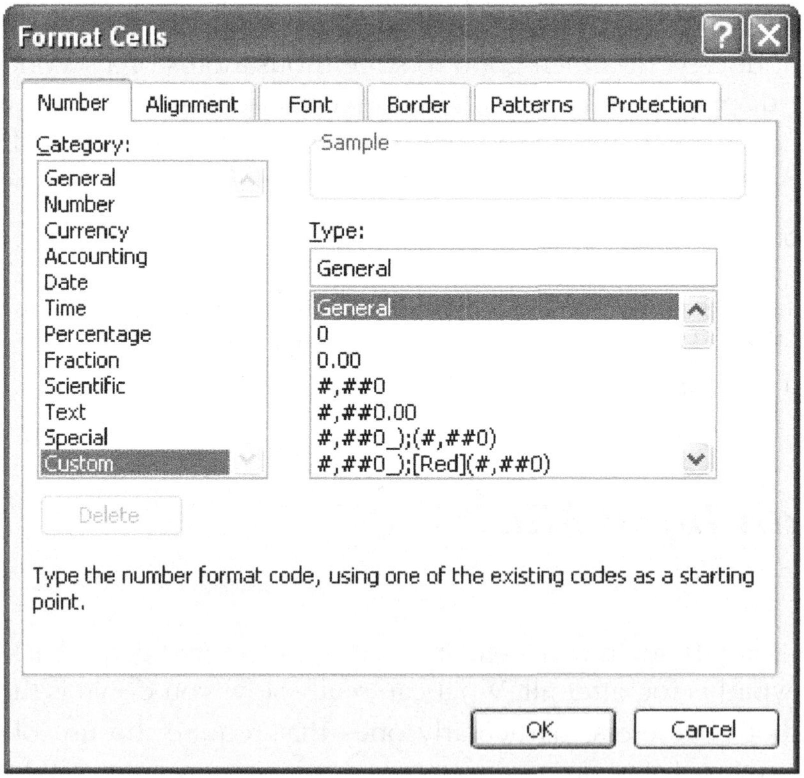

The Number tab of the Format Cells dialog box.

5. Replace whatever is in the Type box with **#":"00** (a pound sign, quote mark, colon, quote mark, and two zeros).

6. Click on OK.

You can now enter your times using just digits. The problem (and this is the bad news) is that the cell doesn't really contain a time. If you enter 230 (for 2:30), it doesn't contain 2:30 as a time—it contains two hundred and thirty. Thus, you can't use the contents of the cell directly in time calculations.

To overcome this, you can use another column to show the entered digits converted into a time. All you need to do is use a formula to do the conversions. For instance, if the time you entered was in cell A3, you could use the following formula in a different cell to do the conversion:

```
=(INT(A3/100)/24)+((A3 - (INT(A3/100)*100))/1440)
```

Format the cell that contains the above formula so it displays one of the various time formats, and you are all set.

4

Formatting Techniques and Ideas

Easy Value Hiding

Applies to Excel 97, 2000, 2002, and 2003

Excel provides many different ways to hide the content of your workbooks. Perhaps one of the easiest (and most novel) ways is to use the custom formatting feature of the program. Follow these steps:

1. Select the cells whose content you want to hide.
2. Choose Cells from the Format menu. Excel displays the Format Cells dialog box.
3. Make sure the Number tab is displayed.
4. In the list of format categories, select Custom.

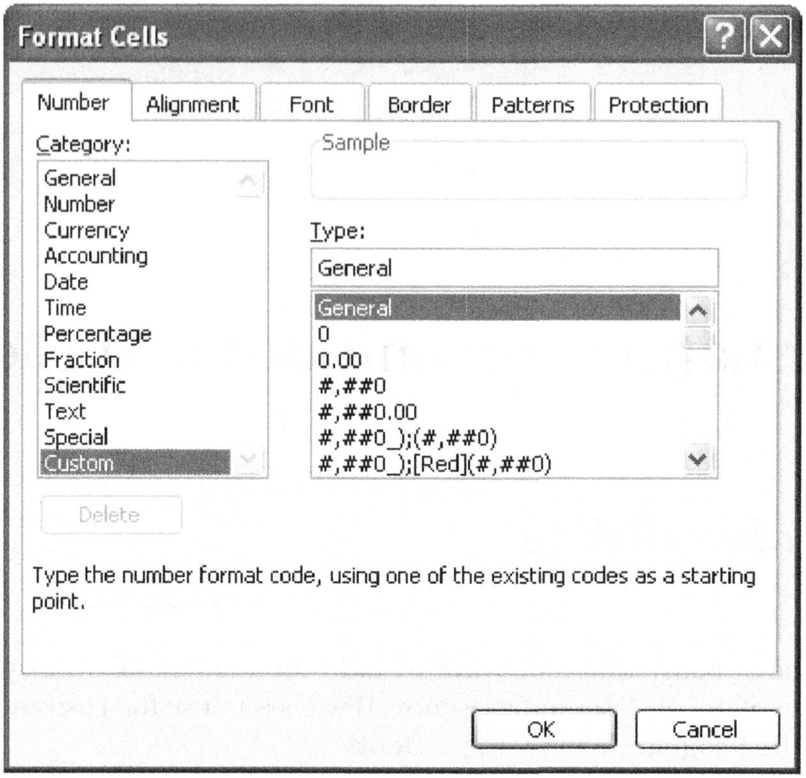

The Number tab of the Format Cells dialog box.

5. In the Type box, enter three semicolons (;;;).
6. Click on OK.

Now the information in the cell is not visible, nor will it print. You can, however, see the information in the Formula Bar, and it can be overwritten if you enter anything else in the cell.

Hiding Individual Cells

Applies to Excel 97, 2000, 2002, and 2003

Ruby has a worksheet that she needs to print out in a couple of different ways, for different users. Part of preparing her data for printing involves hiding or displaying some rows and some columns, as appropriate. Ruby wondered if there was a way to hide the contents of individual cells, as well.

If, by "hide," you want to have the cell disappear and information under it move up (like when you hide a row) or move left (like when you hide a column), then there is no way to do this in Excel. Actual hiding in this manner can only be done on a row or column basis.

There are ways that you can hide the information in the cell, however, so that it doesn't show up on the printout. One easy way, for instance, is to format the cell so its contents are white. This means that, when you print, you'll end up with "white on white," which is invisible. Test this solution, though—some printers, depending on their capabilities, will still print the contents.

If this approach works for you, you could expand on it just a bit to make your data preparation tasks just a bit easier. Follow these general steps:

1. In an out-of-the-way cell (let's say it is cell J1) insert the letter "p."
2. Select the cell (or cells) you want to hide on the printout.
3. Choose Format | Conditional Formatting.
4. Set the conditional format such that if cell J1 is equal to "p," the contents of the cells are white.
5. Print your worksheet as normal. The cell contents should not show up on the printout.
6. To make the cell contents visible on the printout, just modify cell J1 so that it contains something other than the letter "p."

Another solution is to use a custom format for the cells whose content you want to hide. Follow these steps:

1. Select the cell (or cells) you want to hide.
2. Choose Cells from the Format menu. Excel displays the Format Cells dialog box.
3. Make sure the Number tab is displayed.
4. In the list of format categories, select Custom.

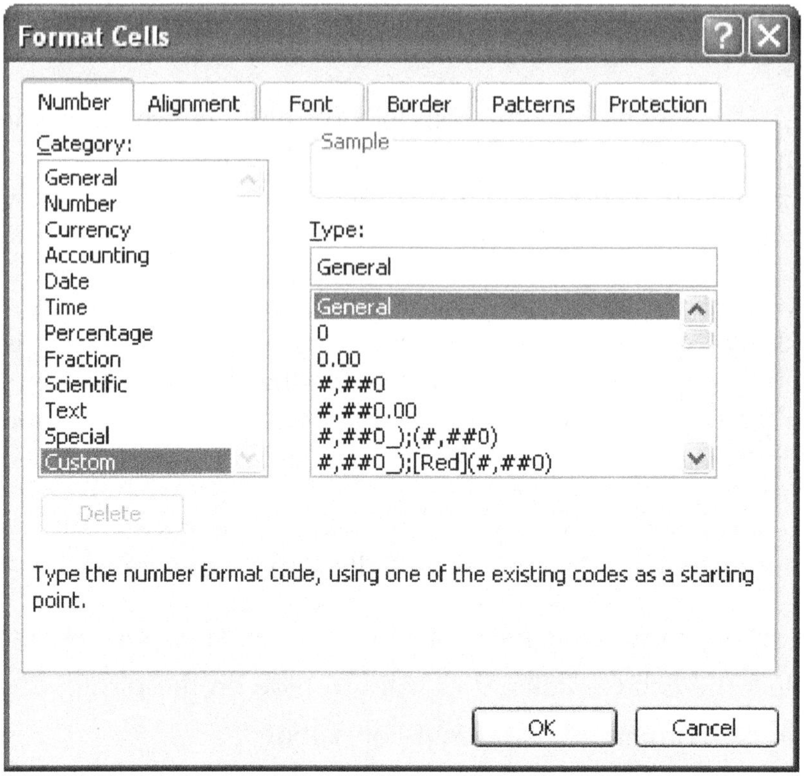

The Number tab of the Format Cells dialog box.

5. In the Type box, enter three semicolons (;;;).
6. Click on OK.

Now the information in the cell is not visible, nor will it print. You can, however, see the information in the Formula Bar, and it can be overwritten if you enter anything else in the cell.

Using a Custom Format to Add Dashes

Applies to Excel 97, 2000, 2002, and 2003

Justin has part numbers that he routinely uses in a worksheet, such as 660501C016971. He would like to apply a custom format to the cell and have the part number automatically displayed with dashes at the proper location, such as 6605-01-C01-6971.

Unfortunately this cannot be done with a custom format. Why? Because custom formats are for the display of numbers, not text. There is one text format, designated by an ampersand, but that is it; there are no others and no others can be defined.

Since custom formats cannot be used, one is left to figure out a workaround. One way to do it is to examine your part numbers and see if the text portion of the number can be removed and the part number still be usable. For instance, Justin's number is 660501C016971. If the format for the part number always calls for the letter C at the same point in the part number (and no other possible letters there), then you could simply delete the C and be left with the number 660501016971. Since it is a number, you can develop a custom format for it that includes dashes in the proper places and the letter C in the proper place. The custom format would look like this:

```
0000-00-C00-0000
```

With the format applied to a cell that contains the number 660501016971, you would end up with a correctly formatted part number displayed: 6605-01-C01-6971. This approach does have drawbacks, however. The biggest drawback is that if you ever want to export the part numbers to another program, perhaps as a CSV file, what ends up exporting is the original number without the formatting or the letter C.

Another workaround is to use a formula to display the part numbers in the format you desire. You could enter them into a cell without dashes, and then use the formula to add the dashes at the appropriate places. When creating reports, then, you would simply hide the column that contains the part numbers without the dashes. Here's a formula that will work, provided the part number without dashes is in cell A1:

```
=LEFT(A1,4) & "-" & MID(A1,5,2) & "-" & MID(A1,7,3) & "-" & RIGHT(A1,4)
```

If you work with the part numbers quite a bit, you might want a way to both add and remove the dashes easily. The best way to do this is with a macro. You can develop a macro that will allow you to add and remove the dashes from a part number in a selected range of cells. The following is an example of such a macro.

```
Sub DashesIn()
    DoDashes ("In")
End Sub

Sub DashesOut()
    DoDashes ("Out")
End Sub

Private Sub DoDashes(What As String)
    Dim c As Range
    Dim J As Integer

    For Each c In Selection.Cells
        If c.Value <> "" Then
            J = InStr(c.Value, "-")
            Select Case What
                Case "Out"
                    While J > 0
                        c.Value = Left(c.Value, J - 1) & _
                          Mid(c.Value, J + 1, Len(c.Value))
                        J = InStr(c.Value, "-")
                    Wend
                Case "In"
                    If J = 0 Then
                        c.Value = _
                          Left(c.Value, 4) & "-" & _
                          Mid(c.Value, 5, 2) & "-" & _
                          Mid(c.Value, 7, 3) & "-" & _
                          Right(c.Value, 4)
                    End If
            End Select
        End If
    Next c
End Sub
```

Note that there are actually three macros in this listing. The first (DashesIn) adds dashes to a part number, while the second (DashesOut) removes them. Simply select the cells containing the part numbers and then run the macro that will perform the operation you want done.

Both DashesIn and DashesOut call the common routine, DoDashes, to actually do the work. The macro examines all the cells in the selection and then performs whatever operation needs to be done on the contents of those cells.

Partially Blocking Social Security Numbers

Applies to Excel 97, 2000, 2002, and 2003

If you have a worksheet that includes Social Security Numbers in it, you may be looking for a way to protect the numbers by only displaying the last four digits. So, instead of displaying 278-43-6128, you would only want to display ***-**-6128.

The way to accomplish this depends, in large part, on whether the Social Security Number is stored in the cell as a number or as text. If the SSN is entered with its dashes (as in 278-43-6128), then Excel stores it as text. If the SSN is entered without dashes (as in 278436128), then Excel stores it as a number.

If the SSN is stored as a number, you may be tempted to create a custom format that hides the first part of the number. Unfortunately, there is no way to do this with a custom format. You could create a custom format that would hide all except the first digits, as in this manner:

```
000,,"-**-****"
```

As you can surmise from this example, custom formats don't allow you to mask out anything except the last portion of any value. Another drawback to this approach, however, is that Excel "rounds" the SSN, such that 277536128 is displayed as 278-**-****.

The best solution to displaying only the last part of a Social Security Number is to use a second column for the actual display. Instead of trying to format the number (or text) itself, it is best to use a formula that refers to the number and creates the desired result. For instance, if the SSN is in cell B7, then you would place the following formula in a different cell:

```
="***-****-" & RIGHT(B7,4)
```

This formula will work with any SSN, regardless of whether it is stored as a number or as text. The other big benefit to this approach is that it allows you to completely hide the original numbers. Even if you were able to use a custom format to hide the first portion of the number (which you can't), someone could still see the SSN in the Formula bar if the cell containing the number is selected.

Using the formula approach, however, allows you to hide the source column, or use sheet protection to hide the contents of the column. This is a big benefit if your goal is to really protect the Social Security Number from prying eyes.

Superscripts in Custom Formats

Applies to Excel 97, 2000, 2002, and 2003

When working in Excel, you can easily format text so that it contains superscripts, subscripts, or whatever other formatting tricks you want. You use the Cells option on the Format menu to make these font modifications. This menu option is not available when you are defining custom formats, however. What if you want to place a superscript in your custom formats?

The answer is to use some of the special font characters available to Windows users. Using these characters you can easily insert superscripted numbers, as long as they are the numbers 0, 1, 2, or 3. Simply use the following shortcuts, where you hold down the **ALT** key as you type the numbers on the numeric keypad:

Superscript	Shortcut
0	Alt+0186
1	Alt+0185
2	Alt+0178
3	Alt+0179

These shortcuts work if you are using the Arial font in your worksheet, which is the default. If you are using some other font, the character codes to create the superscripted numbers may be different. In that case, you will need to use the Windows Character Map accessory to figure out what shortcut keys to use to get the results you want. (On my Windows XP system, I can access the Character Map accessory by choosing Start | All Programs | Accessories | System Tools | Character Map. It may differ on your version of Windows. You may also need to install the Character Map using Windows Setup program if you cannot find it on your system.) When using the Character Map, you can select a symbol and see in the lower-right corner of the program window what the numeric keypad shortcut key is for the character.

Engineering Calculations

Applies to Excel 97, 2000, 2002, and 2003

In an engineering environment, it is not unusual to need to "normalize" numbers in some manner. For instance, you may need to show numeric values normalized to multiples of 10^3, such that 7340 is expressed as 7.34 and 73400 is expressed as 73.4.

It is possible in Excel to use a custom number format to express information in scientific notation that will normalize the display of a number to a multiple of 10^3. To do this, you would follow these steps:

1. Select the cells you want formatted.
2. Choose Cells from the Format menu. Excel displays the Format Cells dialog box.
3. Make sure the Number tab is selected.
4. In the list of format categories, choose Custom.

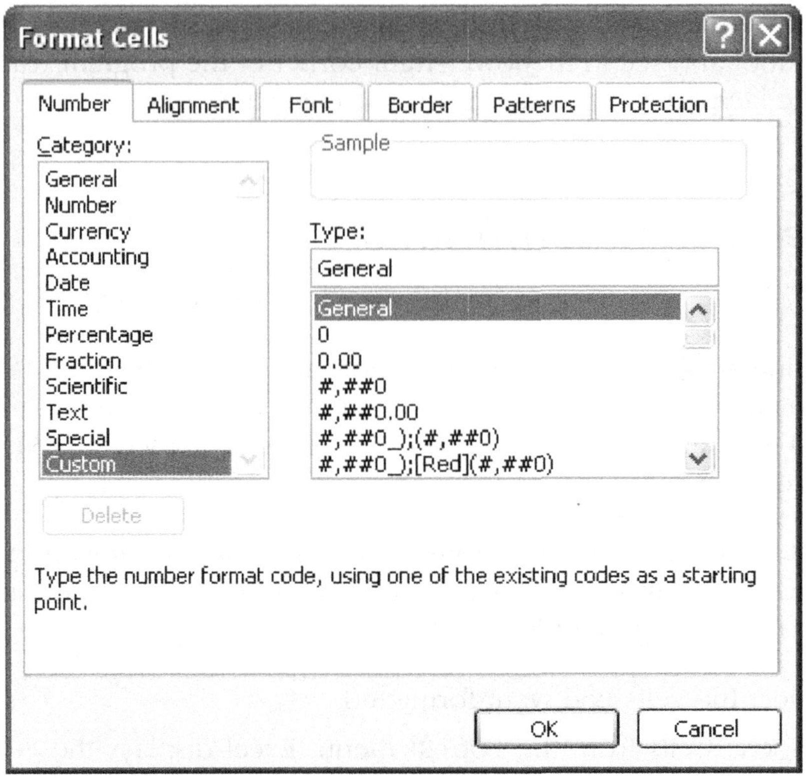

The Number tab of the Format Cells dialog box.

5. In the Type box, enter **##0.0E+0** as your format. (This provides only one number to the right of the decimal place. If you want more, increase the number of zeros after the decimal place.)
6. Click on OK.

Now, when you enter a number such as 7340 into the cell, Excel displays it as 7.3E+3. Because of the way the cell format was entered, the portion after the E will always be a multiple of 3.

This is fine and good, but what if you want just the 7.3 in the cell, and then a metric prefix with a unit in an adjoining cell, such as kilograms? This is a bit more complex, but it can be done using formulas. For instance, let's assume you have your original number in cell A2, you wanted the normalized number in cell B2, and the metic prefix and unit name in cell C2. All you would need to do is enter the following formula in cell B2:

```
=IF(OR(A2>=1,A2<=-1),SIGN(A2)*(ABS(A2)/(10^(3*INT(LOG(ABS(A2))/3)))),
IF(A2=0,0,SIGN(A2)*(ABS(A2)*10^(-3*INT(LOG(ABS(A2))/3)))))
```

Assuming the units you are working with are an imaginary unit called a foo, in cell C2 you would use a different formula, as follows:

```
=IF(OR(A2>=1, A2<=-1),CHOOSE(INT(LOG(ABS(A2))/3)+1, "Foos", "Kilofoos",
"Megafoos", "Gigafoos", "Terafoos", "Petafoos", "Exafoos"),
IF(A2=0,"",CHOOSE(INT(-LOG(ABS(A2))/3)+1, "Millifoos", "Microfoos",
"Nanofoos", "Picofoos", "Femtofoos", "Attofoos")))
```

These formulas may seem a bit long, and they are. However, they will work for any number between approximately -9.99999E-18 to 9.99999E+20. For instance, if you put the number .000125 in cell A2, then cell B2 will contain 125 and cell C2 would contain Millifoos.

If you prefer to not use longer formulas such as these in your workbooks, you can develop a couple of VBA functions to do the trick. The following function, MySciNum, returns a normalized number. Thus, you would use =MySciNum(A2) in cell B2 to get the same results as noted above:

```
Function MySciNum(BaseNum As Double) As Double
    Select Case BaseNum
        Case Is >= 1
            While Abs(BaseNum) > 1000
                BaseNum = BaseNum / 1000
            Wend
        Case 0
            'Do nothing
        Case Else
            While Abs(BaseNum) < 1
                BaseNum = BaseNum * 1000
            Wend
    End Select
    MySciNum = BaseNum
End Function
```

This function only returns a number. To return the units with the appropriate metric prefix, you would use the following function. All you need to do is pass it the cell reference and the name of a single unit. For instance, you could use =MySciPre(A2, "foo"). The macro is as follows:

```
Function MySciPre(BaseNum As Double, Unit As String) As String
    Dim OrigNum As Double
    Dim Pref As Integer
    Dim Temp As String
```

```
Pref = 0
OrigNum = BaseNum
Select Case BaseNum
    Case Is >= 1
        While Abs(BaseNum) > 1000
            BaseNum = BaseNum / 1000
            Pref = Pref + 1
        Wend
    Case 0
        Pref = 99
    Case Else
        While Abs(BaseNum) < 1
            BaseNum = BaseNum * 1000
            Pref = Pref - 1
        Wend
End Select

Select Case Pref
    Case -6
        Temp = "atto" & Unit
    Case -5
        Temp = "femto" & Unit
    Case -4
        Temp = "pico" & Unit
    Case -3
        Temp = "nano" & Unit
    Case -2
        Temp = "micro" & Unit
    Case -1
        Temp = "milli" & Unit
    Case 0
        Temp = Unit
    Case 1
        Temp = "kilo" & Unit
    Case 2
        Temp = "mega" & Unit
    Case 3
        Temp = "giga" & Unit
    Case 4
        Temp = "tera" & Unit
    Case 5
        Temp = "peta" & Unit
    Case 6
        Temp = "exa" & Unit
    Case Else
        Temp = ""
End Select

If Len(Temp) > 0 Then
    Temp = LCase(Temp)
    Temp = UCase(Left(Temp, 1)) & Mid(Temp, 2)
    If Abs(OrigNum) <> 1 Then Temp = Temp & "s"
```

```
    End If

    MySciPre = Temp
End Function
```

Inserting a Radical Symbol

Applies to Excel 97, 2000, 2002, and 2003

A *radical* is a mathematical symbol used to denote "roots" of a value. The most common radical is used to denote a square root. The typical method of inserting a radical is to hold down the **ALT** key as you type 251 on the numeric keypad. Release the **ALT** key, and the symbol appears.

Of course, the appearance of the radical (or even whether it appears at all) depends on the font used in the cell. The **ALT+251** method works for most normal fonts, but some fonts may not include the radical symbol (in which case it won't appear) or may have the symbol mapped to a different position in the font. In that case, the best way to insert the symbol is to use the Symbol dialog box to search through the desired font and find the radical.

You can also use the Windows Character Map program to find the radical, copy it to the Clipboard, and then paste it into Excel. (You can locate the Character Map program by choosing Start | All Programs | Accessories | System Tools | Character Map. This works in Windows XP, but may not work in other versions of Windows.)

All of the methods described so far are great if the only thing you want in the cell is the radical. You can, however, format a cell so that the radical symbol is displayed just to the left of whatever value is in the cell. Perhaps the easiest way to apply this format to a cell is to use a macro, as shown here:

```
Sub Radical()
    ActiveCell.NumberFormat = ChrW(8730) & "General"
End Sub
```

Select the cell you want to format, then run the macro. (You can see how this custom format is handled by Excel if you run the macro and then display the Format Cells dialog box.)

Adjusting Cell Margins for More White Space

Applies to Excel 97, 2000, 2002, and 2003

Serena asked if there is a way to adjust the text margins with a cell so that there is more white space within a cell. The answer is that there is no intrinsic Excel command to add more space, as you can do in Word tables or with the CELLPADDING attribute in an HTML table. However, there is a way you can accomplish the desired goal, although it is somewhat more manual in nature. Follow these general steps:

1. Select the cell you want to adjust.
2. Choose Cells from the Format menu. Excel displays the Format Cells dialog box.
3. Make sure the Alignment tab is displayed.

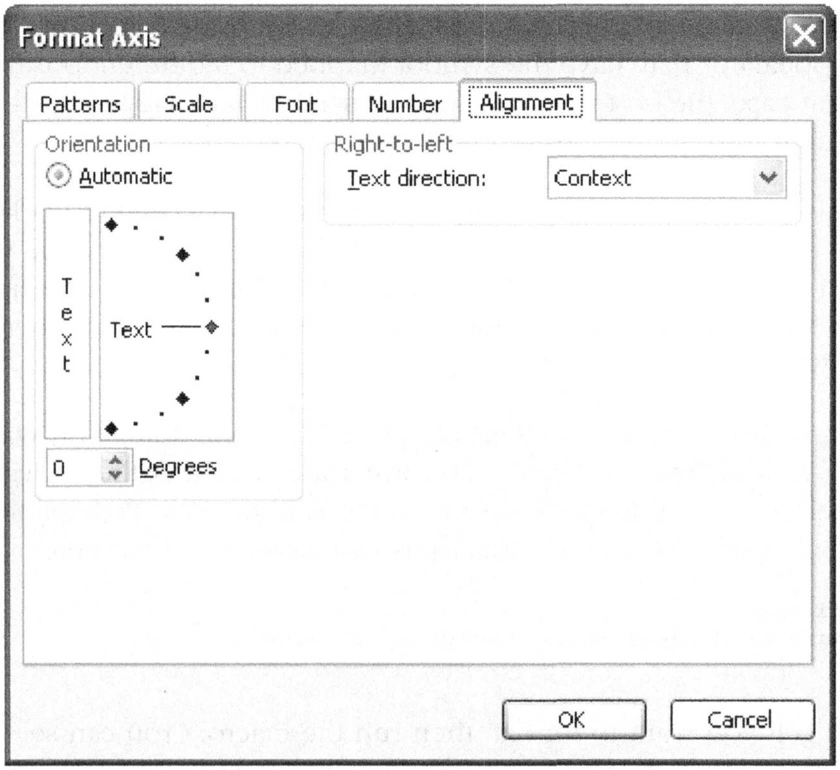

The Alignment tab of the Format Cells dialog box.

4. Using the Horizontal drop-down list, choose Center.
5. Using the Vertical drop-down list, choose Center.
6. Click on OK.
7. Adjust your column width to leave the desired white space on both sides of the cell contents.
8. Adjust your row height to leave the desired white space above and below the cell contents.

The drawback to this approach, of course, is that it affects the width of not just one cell, but of the entire column and row. In addition, your numbers will not line up properly—on the decimal point—if you choose to center horizontally. The way around this last issue is to still center the contents horizontally, but use a custom number format for the cells, as follows:

```
[???,??0.00;-??,??0.00]
```

The question marks in the format forces Excel to leave space as if there were a digit, even if there isn't.

You cannot change the vertical white space without adjusting row height. There is, however, one thing you can try if you want to change the horizontal white space: Adjust the indent value used in a cell. All you need to do is display the Format Cells dialog box, and then set the indent on the Alignment tab. If you are using Excel 97 or 2000 you can only adjust the left indent. If you are using a later version of Excel you can adjust either the left or right indent (check out the Horizontal drop-down list), but not both.

Labeling X-Y Scatter Plots

Applies to Excel 97, 2000, 2002, and 2003

Martin has a worksheet containing 50 rows of data, each row describing a single object. Column A contains the name of the object, column B contains its X coordinate, and column C contains its Y coordinate. When he creates an X-Y scatter chart (column B against column C) the result, as desired, is a graph showing an array of points showing the location of the objects. However,

Martin can't seem to label the data points with their individual names (from column A). When he tries to label the data points the only available options are to label each point with its X value, Y value, or Series Name. Martin wonders if there is a way he can easily use Column A to label the plotted data points.

This can be done manually, but it is tedious at best. For 50 rows it would quickly be brutal, so it is best to look at a macro-oriented approach. One idea is to use a macro similar to the following, which steps through the data points in the X-Y chart and reads the label values from column A.

```
Sub DataLabelsFromRange()
    Dim Cht As Chart
    Dim i, ptcnt As Integer

    Set Cht = ActiveSheet.ChartObjects(1).Chart
    On Error Resume Next
    Cht.SeriesCollection(1).ApplyDataLabels _
      Type:=xlDataLabelsShowValue, _
      AutoText:=True, _
      LegendKey:=False

    ptcnt = Cht.SeriesCollection(1).Points.Count
    For i = 1 To ptcnt
        Cht.SeriesCollection(1).Points(i).DataLabel.Text = _
          ActiveSheet.Cells(i + 1, 1).Value
    Next i
End Sub
```

The macro assumes that the first row of the worksheet contains header information and that the actual data begins in row 2. If the data really begins in row 1, then change "i + 1" to simply "i". (This macro approach is actually a variation of a macro found on pages 570-571 of John Walkenbach's excellent book *Excel 2003 Power Programming With VBA*.)

One rather unique non-macro approach is to use Excel's custom formats. All you need to do is set up a bunch of custom formats that contain only the text you want to be displayed. For example, if you have the values Age, 15, and 23 in cells A3 to C3, you can format either cell B3 or C3 to show the word "Age" even though the value will remain 15 or 23, respectively. Just enter "Age" (including the quotation marks) for the Custom format for the cell. Then format the chart to display the label for X or Y value.

When you do this, the X-axis values of the chart will probably all changed to whatever the format name is (i.e., Age). However, after formatting the X-axis to Number (with no digits after the decimal in this case) rather than General, the chart should display correctly.

This approach can obviously still take a bit of time to implement as you set up and apply a bunch of custom formats for each value in your data series. If you don't want to mess with writing and testing your own macros or creating a bunch of custom formats, you can always turn to add-ins written by others. Microsoft MVP Rob Bovey has created an excellent (free) add-in for Excel which includes an X-Y labeling feature among several others. It can be downloaded at this address:

```
http://www.appspro.com/Utilities/ChartLabeler.htm
```

Excel 2003 Serious Sorting

Using Excel you can manage data in a variety of ways with a number of tools. One commonly used Excel tool is embodied within its sorting capabilities. Excel allows you to easy and quickly sort data in just about any manner you can conceive.

Even though sorting data may be a routine task in Excel, many people still don't have a firm grasp on how to use the program's sorting capabilities fully. Even those who have been using the program for years and years often get into a rut and fail to recognize or take advantage of the full sorting power inherent in Excel.

Excel 2003 Serious Sorting discusses how you can use all the sorting capabilities provided in Excel, perhaps in ways you've never before considered.

ExcelTips: The Macros

Want to master Excel and make it adapt to what you want done? Then you need to discover the power of macros. Macros are a great way to expand the utility of Excel and the ways you can use the program.

ExcelTips: The Macros is designed for those wanting to learn how to create, use, and expand their understanding of Excel macros. In its pages you uncover how to make your use of Excel even more productive. It is the largest, most in-depth exploration of macros available anywhere!

Powerful Lookup Functions

Excel provides hundreds of worksheet functions you can use to build formulas, modify data, and get just the information you need in a cell. Of all the worksheet functions available, few are more powerful than Excel's lookup functions. They literally allow you to "look up" information based upon parameters you specify.

The pages of *ExcelTips: Powerful Lookup Functions* focus on dozens of tips that can help you better understand not only what lookup functions are, but how to use them in real-world scenarios to improve the calculations you must do in your own workbooks.

Times and Dates

Many people use Excel to enter, process, calculate, format, and display dates or times. *ExcelTips: Times and Dates* is designed to help you figure out just what to do with the times and dates stuck in your worksheets. No matter how you need to work with dates and times, *ExcelTips: Times and Dates* can help you out.

tips .NET

Stay in Top Form!

If you want to stay in top Excel form, consider subscribing to *ExcelTips*. Your subscription is free; all you need is an e-mail account and you can receive a weekly dose of tips related to Excel. To subscribe, just visit the *ExcelTips* Web site:

`http://excel.tips.net`

If you prefer to only consider tips that work with Excel 2007 or Excel 2010, then you'll want to visit our website that focuses on those versions:

`http://excelribbon.tips.net`

ExcelTips is part of the Tips.Net network, a collection of websites designed to bring you helpful tips, tricks, and ideas that can save you time, effort, and money. You can see the full breadth of the Tips.Net network by visiting our website:

`http://www.tips.net`

Visit http://store.tips.net for more great Tips.Net titles!

Made in the USA
Monee, IL
08 November 2026

67816243R00039